A Word in Your Fear

Poems by John Doyle

Kung Fu Treachery Press
Rancho Cucamonga, CA

Copyright © John Doyle, 2024

First Edition: 1 3 5 7 9 10 8 6 4 2

ISBN: 978-1-958182-54-3

LCCN: 2023951373

Cover and author photos: John Doyle

Acknowledgments

Some of these poems appeared in the following websites and publications - *The Rye Whiskey Review, Lothlorien Poetry Journal, Fevers of the Mind*

My gratitude to the editors for their support.

Table of Contents

Thank you all, especially YOU

Lightfoot : *Now what the hell is that? a prayer?*
John Doherty : *a poem.*

-Thunderbolt and Lightfoot, 1974

St. Blaise Taught Me How To Sing the Blues

The house-band's name suggests support act - eternally;
I heard it's an urban myth worms become two separate
    beings
when chopped in half, maybe Walt Whitman said that,

maybe it was Dorothy Parker.
"I did little on the Sabbath" I told my boss on Monday-
"held up Wells Fargo, shot that Bannerman leaving
    church,

made Marcus Aurelius question everything he'd
    learned", little else, I told him;
I see him slumped in a fugue state at the water-cooler,
Sunday means not that much to me.

There's a stallion weeping in subterranean seasons,
what he keeps me alive for I don't know,
Lord, oh mighty Lord, I am low on temperance and
    good cheer today.

There's a body in this house un-built, rusting, blood
    turning to steamy potions;
top on Frank Lloyd Wright's diary entry
for the year of our Lord, whenever - is this house might
    come to life -

there's a dream tomorrow night
of me sleeping with a cactus-tree for a friend,
it's Friday night's movie show that shapes bricks without
    mortar

in an angel's flint and sulfur head,
there's a box outside a general store in 19th century
    badlands,
inside the box lies a body, a sign says "killers beware,"

inside the head of the body in the box are dreams of
    houses built,
children on faraway hills, faceless - faceless but fast and
    moving.
That stallion stopped weeping when he'd seen me

learning to read and write
with a blind-man's lonely and depraved daughter,
the stallion knew Aurelius had something,

something they could bottle and take in their wagons to
    Kansas.
The sky looks mostly like it was
when I was a millionaire - *Levis* blue, lazy, content -

as sometimes I watched Alan Ladd from yearly paces,
how he crushed through crispy pine
becoming man at the corpse-chilled hissing stream,

no creature's tenure short nor lost of meaning.
I watched him weave like a wizard, leaving his wallet -
made from the skin of Satan - on that rock of ages

in the curtained loom of weakened smoke, that man of
    chiming centuries.
Fatso with a sawn-off appeared from behind to blast me
    away,
I saw his numerous chins ripple on that breeze,

I finished his epitaph cousin Samuel started typing in 1891,
a dead man's face seeping tomorrow from my fingers.
It didn't bother him for many years

that every man was called his brother, every sister was
    his brother too,
his mother was his brother when jury duty came
    a-knockin,
his father was nothing to him though, watching B-Movies
    murder A-Movie stars

and touching himself inappropriately
as Grizzly wrestled mom for a dollar's worth of garbage
    - oh! how his lover laughed…
It didn't bother me

that for many years I was a coward; setting crickets free
from boxes at the general store was until then
my one achievement travelling writers took note of.

Leaving my carriage, I see her kind face and honest eyes
    and say goodbye.
Alexandria told me her lover had shaved off all he had,
this upset her, so she left his dowry and unkindness
    behind;

Alexandria's kind face and honest eyes -
how could any man do that to her?
Her family will purchase a plot of land, she said,

they plan to build a new hotel,
bring something to this town that may please the
almighty, something mentioned on page twenty-six

in the book of Saint Blaise
who taught me how (and when)
to sing the blues. I holler back to Alexandria

as I jump from the moving carriage,
I tell her I can sing the blues,
that I'm pretty sharp these days on the upright piano...

North

Why go that way?
We never make much headway jumping ships
southerly-bound, west, even turning east that faulty old
    Friday.
Naturally you blame those waters it lumbers on,
hours were something a clock held against you,
days were something you couldn't fill,
unless death had said something to a long-lost uncle you
    never knew,
but did right then, in a fit of life's last rite - making you
    something to be cherished
at his ceremony of the worms - "oh how do you do, you
    must be the youngest, oldest, no?"
Why go any way?
Well, I say, up north there's gold and wine, and songs
    and dreams,
there are things no other part of you has yet bled for,
lest your blood be real, and the compass be a knife
willing to cut your guts right open one last time.
North it is - alone, a slivered jab of freedom tingling
on a baggy-eyed clock -
near that screaming city.
Hear that city scream, feel its heat,
measuring us like that wicked old compass your uncle
    burned into rubies

And Billy Tells Rose-Marie

And Billy tells Rose-Marie how well he'll treat her
stopping to water daffodils he missed, Tuesday spots
    these indiscretions like no other,
Rose-Marie tells Billy how well Herb and Joe and Nurse
    Douglas treated her,
stopping to pull back her curtains to see if her National
    Geographic has arrived,
Jackie telling Mattie how well he'll treat her,
holding Rose-Marie's favourite roses
at a dank-white wooden porch
across from a railroad halt Spencer Tracy nearly got off at

Jazz

Someone was right, someone calls it the Devil's music,
it's true Davis hasn't paid my bills,

Monk doesn't put my eats in my gut,
Cannonball smiles from a shelf at my tap-grey head

much to Brubeck's amusement.
Someone calls this Devil's music,

so far today, I've put five coffees away
wrapped up in sorrows of Chet Baker's choosing,

making me wonder where
did the beauty turn to grief, why is Sinatra always losing?

Minnesota Dirt Road Song

That moment when dusk
accepted its defeat -
new year fireworks simmering

a single shotgun salute,
curtain calls dangling from a tree
like a mob left town an hour ago -

the horses' hooves
went-off like fireworks in
a ranch burning like a dying star,

dust an answer to a fable
tyre-tracks moaned,
after leaving church three minutes too early

The European Girls Who Walked Down
the Streets in the Rain

Never knew that from my room
I heard less than anything I saw,
because though I knew they were out there somewhere,

they never knew that from my room
I'd pictured how much rain it would take
to make their mothers and their fathers

appear on local news headlines
wondering how long it would take for waters to subside
and for me to come down from my tower

parting waters that washed their only child away,
moments after being told she'd been accepted into
college.
The European girls knew nothing, they were shadows
    saved in pavement cracks

until flooded streets
washed my sinful mind
free of its need to be a local hero

The Cars Move Way Too Fast on the Boulevard
After I Leave That Bar on 4th Avenue

A hotshot lawyer working out of 2nd Avenue

tells
me

they've tuned their transsexual

sisters' radio into air pollution

unlearning a follow up day

they

pull a grey skies

four or more wheeled highway

menace gone nowhere nothing

goodbye, phhhhtttt!!
The hat on my head is a reasonable rhyme

my brain dug into hours that left the clocks

collars and handcuffs

aghast.

Sometimes

    you show me love

        like the halved reasons of scarecrow

sitting in their

    bar brawl mathematics, some called Matthew,

        some called away to dubious duty
      on a wing of a

          tragedy,

    a turbine tailored prayer, sometimes
      you want dinner,
    so I

        follow lunchtime's

chessboard

    epiphany.

 I am the parking space loser, the stiffened sailing
silhouette of the far away angel

         thumbing

back to his

    siphoned segmented Cadillac

in a day and

a night soon to come

thumbing

on the side of the thumbprint
hostage Sunday

bare tree circus dimension

ripped and

shredded

pizza-joint road

Working People Go Home Every Evening in Belfast

I am like a drop of water on a rock...
-Rigoberta Menchú

Belfast's middle-classes control a section of highway that
    remains steadfastly neutral,
football stadium roofs remain isolated from words,
thoughts, sinful deeds that may send us a time-capsule
we formed a human-chain to keep buried -
in perpetuity.
Working-classes check messages on mobile phones, on
    railway lines
clicking their purpose into jigsaw-pieces of city-scape
mountain-side used to keep under lock and key,
messages that tell them illness has passed, illness has come,
messages yet to be seen in cars
that pass on roads that know better than iron-horse relics,
swimming in the sonic sermons of evening's promise,
on waves and waves
the skeleton dug into the mountain proclaims.
Everyone in Belfast knows this, me a stranger who listens
    from purgatory,
not too pushed about that green, orange, and stoic-red
    that slows me into all their collages

Hospitals

Usually I don't like
hospitals.
Not places for me, bleachy-drone going on, a genie in
      reverse squeezing into my nose,
my stomach, the hinterlands of my weedy, sand-soft guts.

I usually don't like hospitals.
But, south of the city, there are hospitals I've seen
where people, when past the points of reason, go to.
      Hospitals where Perry Como plays
on respectable local-radio, rugby results are called out,

nurses refer to next of kin as *Lorcan*, as *Fiona*.
Hospitals, after we pass that velvet economic border,
make that land south of concrete utopia
seem like places I'd like to pass on to Jesus from;

rugby-Sundays
back in 1988,
when Grandad had sound and vision
safely swirling from his fingertips, the bedside window
      closed beside him, just to be sure

The Groovy Gang From the Liberal Arts
College Drama Society

She told that boy she'd get him shots,
she didn't mean Neil Young on the CD player, she didn't
    mean penicillin.

She sang the *Star-Spangled Banner* to get the barkeep's
    attention,
he was busy learning how to make himself deaf;

the girls wear their "ironic" mom jeans because their
    bodies are free,
their minds belong to Instagram, Tik Tok, mostly,

a little bit of sinew belongs to themselves.
Deeply and madly uneasy, a lady beside me orders
    tomorrow on the rocks,

later tonight we'll steal a policeman's car, get married
    in the rain.
You need to quit being sober my guardian angel says,

my wife of 48 minutes leaves me to return to real estate
so she can donate her body to science.

After I've flushed the can a student
tells me he doesn't believe I support his ambitions,

I say that I'm hurting on the inside everyday,
doesn't that count?

He said, oh no it doesn't, get a job you gun-totin' hawk,
these are postmodern times.

Your pantaloons are quite horrific sister,
if you don't mind me saying so,

as you sing a song from the withered-jaws of an
    unconscious century;
That sister, I bare you no ill-will for

Martyrdom in E-Minor

Soiled hangs the rag of day out over this town
-John Berryman

Mother Maria, a million others might - no -
would tip their lighted ash east-side of
Roman numerals, this computer-torn mirage
haunting itself into water, mud, this bonfire of prayer

divided by the sum itself into our town's last hope -
    you, Mother Maria,
a million others light their cigarettes
standing in the shapes of the oil-wagons, boxcars,
    burned-down I.T. departments
that make them holier than prayer or fable believes,

climbing into the war-torn womb of our suburbs, hale,
    hearty,
little men in smaller suits whose throats are trapped on
    sinks
pouring bleach across their camouflage of skull-pounded
    bone
to become disciples,

misers to your disbelief;
Mother Maria, my barbed-wire rosaries are two-prong
    electrocutions
daring, pleading,
pouring blood from the stones in the milk

Cheyenne Eight Times

For Dave Walker

A priest asks if animals have souls,
the city asks if its neon knows any virgins on 4th
    and 15th,

the water stopped short of kissing its sea,
worried its land would turn bone-dry, cindered, and
    pointless.

Here's a face, its name sticks like gum on sidewalks
to tax-returns and headstones,

a life is there somewhere, clinging to it,
sipping water at the office cooler

telling other beings of last nights crises,
like the city's neon-tanned virgins,

the animals chasing balls with St. Francis,
the flood that soon comes, the land a sorry sack of bones.

Inside the womb of Santa Rosalita
I watched that remake of *Stagecoach* from 1966.

Things that begin, end,
or do not exist

are matters outside forces can stamp and file.
Inside the womb of Santa Rosalita

I've heard Mike Connors say *Cheyenne* eight times now,
in that remake of Stagecoach, from 1966

Song for John Belushi

Stinking socks
narcotics,
broken plates
cheeseburger serenade,
teardrops
gaining hope,
heartbeat
irregular
mounting bills,
torn-up scripts,
final day
normal street,
too normal.
They play rock n'roll in Heaven the greengrocer
   (who stays nameless to protect the guilty) told him,
it could have been an invite,
a way of luring him in,
heaven as a spider's web he needed to be cuckolded in

Observations

Steve Prefontaine did not see the follow-up to *The
     Man With the Golden Gun.*
This was impossible in a realm where mortality exists.
To date, it remains so.
Man has cloned sheep, made paper-money nearly
     redundant,
got tired very easily of walking on the moon.
There are things though, even the logical, those who
     deny or accept Christ's divinity,
will all accept are impossible.
To learn of Steve's solution,
one must follow a similar path, onwards from this war
     of skin fighting bacteria,
mouth fighting mind, all troubles we are faced with that
     are no doubt somehow, if indirectly,
connected to original sin.
Onwards we must go to learn such things.
It is only when we get there, we know we cannot return,
unless our light comes from a mountain that sometimes
     snarls at the sun at its most easterly.
If so, then all sequels are perfectly possible,
different skin fighting those same germs,
a mouth the shape of something else fighting dialects it
     once denied

Metamorphosissisisyphus

I dreamed I saw St. Elsewhere last night,
a good man who could saw through a knot in wood
    told me
I wasn't a good man or even average man,

I used dynamite to speed up the process
and made him look stupid
in front of Colonel Ethan Rogers, who came in on the
    caboose from Carson City,

he gave me a backhanded compliment for my ingenuity,
    that Colonel Rogers,
a back-hand with a knuckle-duster across my nose.
I dreamed I saw St. Johnstone and St. Mirren last night,

a town without a railway is like a body without a soul,
Mimi Farina died from cancer today,
flat-chested boys sat by fountains near Tuscany in cut-
    off Levis,

they knew it wasn't 1983,
their tears made up for summer's selfish tongue
telling lies about women who died, leaving me all alone
    by a burning bush,

blood turning that fountain October-black.
The trouble with Charles Dickens is that he's too
    Dickensian,
notes our financial advisor,

I handled it like a pro
Delvecchio says,
fixing gloves for his round of squash,

telling everyone
that security guard
won't ask him for I.D. ever again.

The Scandinavian noir drama everyone is talking about
these days, would've been my way in on this gang-bang,
then when I looked up

they were shoveling muck across my casket.
Holy Moses McGinty,
my life sure did go away from me pretty fast

Joe

Some night you'll switch off that light,
some morn that river will wash clean a bleached-out
dawn,

some year that wheel will find its sister missing,
some brother will find nothing but a song shaking off
    mud at your red-bridge crossroads,

some man's wheels and some man's dreams
buckled by these same apparitions,

some morning that light switched off
its night, its river laughing at your dried-out dawn

Olivia

Spain registers neither disinterest -
nor apathy - this means
two things -
one : that your imminent passing

has not yet reached Andalusia
through urgent wires crossing citadels,
those white-washed towns you brought knowledge to,
immersed in a post-mortal blur;

two : those newspapers sectioned-off near your bed
tremble at thoughts of your passing -
when they reach Spain, talk of *Señorita Olivia*
won't clatter itself in shells of sadness,

nor plates empty on cantina tables,
rather, there will be an encore of children pouring
from village schools, days will return to 1961,
though there is darkness in the souls of this mud,

Señorita Olivia makes magic with her chalk
and blackboard, brings narratives of northerly lands.
News will reach them, Olivia -
I stand as your casket-makers howl past me;

I will tell them -
it will be a song,
perhaps a dream,
though - I'll tell them - *Olivia picks oranges from the
tallest trees in our village*

Gluaiseacht : Tríd an Oíche, Tríd an Lá

Níl tine mé.
Níl eagla orm roimh uisce.

Níl olc orm, shiúil mé míle bliain maithiúnais
chun gach fear a chruthú mícheart.

Is gach rud mé,
agus níl aon rud ionam,

mar idir an saol agus idir an bás is ainm mé
a chuireann na réaltaí a sholas ar

Choose Words Carefully, Someday They'll Get Washed Away

Let silence be something -
a thing of note -

a metaphor, perhaps,
which bounds and gags passengers to their emporium
     of seats.

Rivers 20,000 ft below
are made from voices

more-so than water; a junkie's pleas turned to sweat,
the streams of veins

gurgling like babies.
The flight attendants

chat about the last hotel they stayed in,
it was Dortmund, it was late,

little being said at dinner that night,
speech patterns like bullets from the fuselage,

the waters of an entire continent
gossiping like chickens for days -

everyone, everything -
strapped-in tightly

like straps around a junkie's arm.
Everything else

is silent
except planes overhead, strapped-in like babies in the
heavens

Song for Elvin Jones

Mr. Elvin Jones

grooves like a

hornet's nest

next to me on my pc screen,

like a rattlesnake

on caffeine

rummaging   through trash cans in a typhoon.

It is one of my favourite things

that Mr. Elvin Jones

is particles

assembled from the same cosmos as me

Song for Tony Williams

Listening to "In a Silent Way" January 2023

Picasso's rain is falling on the stones -
you want it any other way?
fire hammering mallets on the laughter of the waters?
Tony Williams' wrists on his high-hat, during the moon-
    landings on Jupiter

in 1969? The end of times closes in like a wolf, the rain
    eases off,
which gives us our breakthrough, our supersonic
    confession box,
Padre DeNapoli's
ticket to San Diablo's 52-card showdown.

There's no possible way, we agree, to squeeze blood from
    the stones,
though, we'd try, if there was music trapped in them.
There's music in a jackal's blood, damnation in a
    sidewinder's spit,
jazz is our fire-alarm, Tony Williams tonight is our fire.

The Chrysalis

(1)
Door-keys chime on drain-lids
a parting rite of sorrow
- *Sunderland 0, Hull City 0* -
seven minutes, then October's cease,
footprints spooked in taxi headlights - souls emptied in
full-time whistles

(2)
Sound of gravel
spending dimes and nickels - in sepia,
cinematography vast, sometimes wicked -
Daniel Lanois hides out from lawmen here -
somewhere.

(3)
The caves echoing and music's pools of water,
eternal, somewhat mapped - only moonlight for the next
200 miles,
a rich astral blue, a stone-clenched starlight that scratches
the skin
and pours blood from the music,
sloping light, parched horses stretched like rope.

(4)
In hot pouncing rain
and the sickness
of cloud formations -
weekdays await the one,
Sunday is awaiting the healer

Mise-en-scène

"And yesterday I saw you kissing tiny flowers/ But all that lives is born to die"
-Led Zeppelin "That's the Way", 1970

I saddled up outside Shady's Lounge,
saw some slaphead from behind -
thought it was Rosewall Hensley;
I slithered into the bar in lieu of such a revelation,

surprised I was still fastest on the draw;
another soldier wept there, hammered like a nail
sleeping underneath a train,
I almost re-introduced myself, then Hensley walked in -

it was the wrong slaphead I'd incriminated
sitting in the lounge -
"Real Joe Mannix shit, this is turning out to be", says the
    editor of the *Skid Row Inquirer,*
looking up from Hell. The slaphead I'd be firing blanks at

sits beside Maria Ramirez,
the local queen of jitterbugs and Fall-Time roses,
telling her every reason never to think about winning an
    Oscar, for every script
she misquotes from - he seems like a pleasant fellow,
    maybe a tad curt -

she seemed like Esuvia
when she wrote down on college notepaper her path to
    Broadway,

forgetting how many times x featured in extreme,
forgetting how to spell subtle - when her ma tattooed a
    vicious alphabet across her brother's cot.

I'll get a dream out of this
if I ever teach myself the wicked sin of sleep,
my Tai Chi guru's pulling out his hair
from a window upstairs somewhere,

squeezing blood from the broken-shouldered moon;
a man, who for many years to come
will burn his trigger finger
on luke-warm and clueless light bulbs,

light-bulbs brighter
in glare and substance,
than that thing I knew
as Rosewall Hensley's head

Australian Postage Stamp, 1976 :
Richmond Bridge

Oblivion marks nothing by mortar or mortality alone,
nor its need to conquer by proxy;

Crossing steely waters, we seize our stomach-splat browns
hoarding lights, structures,

a minty-green horizon,
a word of Godliness, a virtue valor firmly weathers inside,

crossing the waters
Protestant, European blue;

Do the souls of the ancients
turn to faces pressed on glass,

making song and sound and sorrow
turn oblivion to this frosty adolescent water?

Time is as helpless as the clock
that betrayed it,

native souls being the last to know such moments,
such shallow water

Manuelo Finnegan

Pappy burned those wrinkled greens
I'd intended to drink mostly, the rest I'd keep safe for
    gambling and for whores.
My voice box for my cancer interfered

with the tv set above the bar.
Everyone thought it was a gas
'til I walked past as the Jets kicked for a last minute
    field-goal

against the Redskins and their universe turned black.
"Isn't all of eternity black?" I said,
after I'd picked my face and teeth from the kerb.

My cousin Bernardo down in Durango owns a pick-up
    truck;
I'll sleep in the back under the stars,
tell Pappy I'm starting a fresh new life in some college

named after some cat who cheated on his wife and died
    from emphysema.
Some time ago
Bernardo told me he'd hit Vernon Presley across the
    head,

stole his wallet, bought a jukebox
and drank nothing but Cajun rum. I knew he was lying,
Vernon went to meet Jesus in '79,

Bernardo didn't touch a drop
until NASA arrived on Pluto in 2795.
The rooks sit here at the Sicilian bakery

watching sunrise play
her withered ice-cube aces first,
then eat what Bernardo's boss left for the Irish;

"the haunted wreck of the nation-state
ain't no place for homesteaders, sandbaggers,
one-eyed jacks and lesser-eyed cats", I tell pappy,

putting the phone back to the receiver
after a lady barely five feet high
taps her imitation pistol Zippo on the phone-booth glass.

I looked at her wheels
as I walked away,
I just knew it would be a Plymouth Fury;

I never said anything to her
about her engine still running.
Let the devil tell her on Sunday morning

A Word in Your Fear

From torrents of this Earth
we choose our day,
at 5am trains slip like eels
from Ballina's jellied womb

as we watch
out of breath,
an immortal outlined
in exhaust pipe fumes.

A man could sneak some fruit
from these trees,
take aim at a few
dusk-cheating birds

The Liminal Figures

For John Compton

A solitary man occupies the mirror-ball
on Friday nights, shattered like Lacan's infant jigsaws,

his moral aspects perched exact centre -
like a student from France who gatecrashes eyes

halfway through the news,
peacefully protesting armageddon

while a cop halfway up the ranks bashes his head open
     with little fear
of anything else

but further commendation -
time, being, feeling, exact centre like that blackboard

on trade-test transmissions where those two creepy fucks
serve some purpose

more so than freaking out
six year olds with homework on one side,

the psychedelic Seventh Seal, 1967-style, peering from the
     other.
No-one told me any of this, I was the centre of someone's
     world,

I did not fight, I did not hunt, I didn't light fires to ward
    off ice and snow
and the horrors of death's dream within me.

I was the centre of the universe and it made me nothing
when I stood in the centre of the street outside,

expecting all and everything
to stop

and notice.
I was graced that cops were so polite this side of town

Inertia 101

A mattress wedged on skirting board
like iron-lungs,

a moonlit sneer
two of them

lined like smoked mackerel
in a jagged tin

are emphasized by -
Ulick's car parked outside

as if little happened,
except weed, ash-end packed cans of supermarket booze,

a chase across rain-sodden fields doing things
students do on nights like these,

nothing in-between
soggy socks, the stinking inertia

of the inevitable rites of passage
I move my soul to the corner of this bedsit from.

Bridget wakes up early,
tells everyone how she likes to dance,

it was Pan who gave her these gifts,
how she will heal the universe through her art.

These are not the days of wine, Sweet Jehovah,
nor are these the days of roses

Ludocus

We gorged our chainsaws through supper
an hour and fifty-seven spells ago,
the street was drizzly,
but the rain cleared after we hit your favourite bar -

you stayed sober - I thought to myself -
it's my turn to do everything you always do.
Ballinteer : Someone's speaking Irish,
Sunday morning, hungover, my chin perched

on fist, not cupped in hand;
I wish you'd speak Irish just once,
your kith and kin never really cared,
looks bad when those customers arrive,

like I'm some sort of mustached-faced
flared-denim scoundrel,
the only man slurping McArdle's
on that late-night boat to Holyhead;

Jesus,
why do they even care?
And the music I heard a century ago
tips this wheel

closer to oblivion,
tips my God to a stone-carved
forgiveness, that parks cars on the wrong-side
of less-righteous roads, not far from Balinteer

The Lamb Lies Down in Galway

I've walked this block
as Moses did,
as Lennon did,
as Lenin did,
as Aileen Wournos did,
as Patti Smith has not - but may very well will—
as all of them died
and Patti Smith stayed here to cup my breasts in her
    armoury.
I stood still and
noticed
how nothing changes
except lightbulbs, dreams, paints when mixed
which then emit colours I believe are colours
purgatory's passports were painted when it existed and

    by nightfall nothing was left in anyone's will -
except Patti Smith who sings songs around me
and I hide in the stones that
women carried when men fled to far-off lands
pretending to slay dragons

Dennis

I feel sand between my toes,
Dennis arriving home -
brown-paper bags jangle a tune

moonlight scores in turquoise -
there's no-one home,
no-one to scream at him.

His bedroom looks out
on the Pacific ocean,
blue, blue, so bloody blue

Bunifaziu, June 2008

A rogue's gallery drips outside this sanctuary
of saints we ask curtly to validate parking tickets for
    invisible cars,
Rachel consolidated on *Level 10* of the beatification
    shuffle - Rachel you see
might get sick today, let's hedge our bets on single yellow
    lines.
Carrying her peace-corps card, water-gun, cherry-bombs
should she get frisky, she double-parks on a single dream,
smiles for the first time since a year
that had an August, a June, and something else her sister
    spat back at me.
God, these streets are Jack-Frost cold
as we make ourselves anonymous
from that sun divorced from clocks that hunt so viciously
I think Rachel might relapse - *roll those drums,*
    ringmaster, here it comes...
There's a medic hiding here today, his windows sabotaged
in dripping-wet towels from industrial-sized washing
    machines
paid for by mobster silence. Rachel, please don't relapse,
a saint gets an allocated time-slot
just like killers don't choose when they ride the lightning -
though it looks like a sunshower's a-coming, Corsica took
    all it could
and expects us to be just as stoic under this madrigal of
    fussy hail,
an audience of pan-pipes mimicking St. Peter's spiel on
    Carotola,
rumours of Rachel's passing tippexed out of his cue-card...

Light Up Mr. Lightfoot's Stogie

February 16th, 2023

Egg-yolk illuminations please
take me home, those sunshine pricks
which warm up Wicklow's secret highway -

a home I left on 90s Sundays,
which, for their penance, gave me 1970s dreams and
    washed-out dreamers,
escaping bare-chested homily, broken lumps of Saturday's
    men

stitched together - in prayer, fiscal forgiveness.
Nearing Bray, I stitched my past to a celluloid messiah,
who made Sundays that same egg-yolk bright

coming from a mountain that
some cat drove by right past me, in his open-top,
his brother-in-arms slumped to a delirium.

I want in.
I'll give the kid his last-rites,
I'll light up Mr. Lightfoot's stogie from the many loves of
    Jesus,

paint egg-yolk strokes on shards
of peering rock
that veer a slip-road into Greystones

You Really Got Me

A week was born from this -
of weathered tribes on buttoned maps -
your breath to steady me

where wind is lost in branch-whipped creeks,
of dull and leaden lanes, houses empty
where ships are fed scrambled signals -

Rockall, fair to moderate, may lose its identity -
but you look, touching, holding,
the lungs and love and light you give, seeing me to shore

Untitled Poem #32653

Otto fumbles through breakfast-time
at 90 degree angles in an arbitrary manner

which may, or may not be dead centre -
in the spleen and ego of North Dakota.

I expect someone will forgive their wrongdoers,
those who hold grudges will suffer as those who carry
    the burdens

of forgiveness, dirty forks,
newspapers from moments ago, moments we know
    would strangle our youth

in diners in North Dakota, while Otto sits outside now,
free to choose his failings.

House parties in modernist blocks
lead into the throat and vulva of the average unknowns,

he's a hula-hoop rounding Saturn,
tutu dress,

star-dust combined,
the zig-zag calculations,

the screaming throat of lightning
leaving rust-specs sheared

from iron gates
on Gothic churches.

On summer days it's him,
city lights,

flashing cars,
seedy hotels;

a feline family stalk
the diesel-engine smiles

of 60 year old men
called *Texas*

propping up pub counters
underneath reruns

of *Minder*
at 2:31pm on Tuesdays.

No-one knows of him,
my little emerald secrets -

but come looking for me again
and I'll be ready, both barrels loaded

where Jun Fukamachi's *Quark* starts breeding,
purple smoke from lilac cinders stalled -

in elevators,
under floorboards,

subway trains,
the greyness of mild-mannered sidewalk

and the red bricks of truck drivers' dreams
in vehicles not necessarily Kenworths or Peterbilts.

Scene One - there's snowfall, a sudden pistol,
a man called *Mr. McCaffrey* places his palms

across the train tracks
of his wild and withered skull.

Otto's left his car somewhere, jacket across his shoulder,
tie loose, bitch-slapping the breeze - across the knives
    that mark mid-day.

Two out of three seems to be the average failure-rate
for our brave and stoic nation,

where that newspaper burns our tongue and laughs at
    next
in North Dakota.

Traffic's murder, they say. Three people
cast a dice on their highway. It's sudden, and cars slow-
    down.

They look like they fell down from Valhalla - or
    crawled-up
from the underworld,

missing limbs, blood and neon all the same,
the coffee shops and heel-repair bars,

cyclists a vision of speed, fluency,
hard-currency falling from a conveyor belt on top of itself,

the machine begging Taurus and Neptune to let it stop.
People leave their factories, stamp their cards, hop on
    bicycles.

Suddenly they too creep up the inside lane.
Bloody men and smock-dress wives

drive average cars
past the abattoir

on a flight to dreams today with plasma-dried panache,
diaries crucified their flesh-cold misgivings.

The heel-bars and coffee shops close their doors
and a fuzzy lilac-blur

envelopes the shadows of those leaving.
Like me, they stop - watch hybrid creatures

scramble highways
as the cars wait like children at feeding time.

Moonlight is patient.
Sunshine is patient. Neon is not.

Jun Fukamachi swoops and takes me there.
It's January, it's raining, it's 4:39p.m.

Maroon raindrops at dusk
and the electronic heartbeats

of 1980
bring a different shade of blue and purple into the
    unshaved limits of sky.

I rarely see these shades these days.
End of report. 4:40p.m. Otto should be nearing his
    photostat machine just now, coffee boiling.

The Fisherman

Newest of the New Yorks!
Have you fed me your leftovers yet?
You see, I've always been keen on this drive-by Sunday
devilishly delighted by serenades of sunburned newspaper
running from its trails of sad sad mouths mouthing their
    cheese-stretched
alibis from screen to riverside, from bridge of a thousand
    ages, to decrepit
basketball court conjoined in a river of sallow scorn.
That's how my cities work. I don't blame New York alone -
    Paris spat at me so much
I needed doctors' jabs to last me that whole night I spent
planning to lay siege to Notre Dame, London, Dublin,
    Rome, New Delhi -
you're like old friends that worm along at bars, digging,
    digging, deeper
in a hex woodworm chewed through less than an hour ago;
    I know,
I saw on the clock as Nostradamus's horse came second
    last and he blew his brains out.
A pity. He was a good drinking pal, my old Alma Mater,
    new Alma Mater,
as nothing too much matters in the newest of the Old
    New Yorks,
casting your line into the river. Ignoring me.

Love Song for the Year 2019

i.m. Ronnie, Michael, Joan, Eileen

We've surfed asteroids before -
no crystals sparkled like these;
We've strayed from astral spectrums before -

no planets spun like these.
Down, under that boardwalk,
music eases water's chills,

above us airplanes hanging like seeds
that flowers give
to reignite, to coat secondary roads in something

like that stadium shivered
from its lungs in 1978,
Argentina arriving to become immortals,

like now,
trains taking some of this into their own aether,
caramel wind and sand-grain truths

that I bring back to the archangels
at a desk stopwatch-soaked and loitering
with tomorrow's *Le Monde;*

oh, how I wish for anything
but the knowing rain,
the rain that cannot be silent and grazing in its song

when that ewe

gave birth,

and we gathered round, electric in our music

Tixerb Kcuf

I don't care how much money I owe the gas company,
I don't care about that cough I have that hasn't gone
    away,
I don't care my boss told me today other staff's
    concerns about my hygiene,
not concerns expressed to my nearly-shaved face.
I'm sitting here whistling like Steve Cropper
watching Spanish students
laugh and run in hot summer rain - like it's a folk-song
    from 1971,
in love with the molecules of something, everywhere,
    everything

J. Nixon Esquire : Commissioned Portrait
Artist Working Out of Shysterville

He painted by numbers,
sipping Scotch, then dingleberry wine,
then, on turning away from me

he noted "hey hotshot, they've withdrawn my commission
any chance you'd drop me by a bus station sometime?"
I wasn't sure what time was, I'd seen clocks before,

over grease-smudge tiles on diner walls
where Nixon sat side by side with two-thousand other men,
his hat and coat still on, his sass stuck on that luggage rack

of a bus with a wheel as flat as my wine.
He told me his brother's name, "same as Mr. Hart, and
    Mr. Livingston Seagull",
as I put jump-leads to my wine, I turned and asked

"why don't you go and kiss your mirror? your lips taste
    the same as your id and ego's withered vine".
Catching someone else's bus, he painted something new
    by numbers,
turned on his toes when he'd reached the outskirts

of his brother's mind, learning only then I wasn't his
    shotgun rider,
the bullet-holes in his mirror half an hour faster
than the dry-rot that erased the commissions in his ego

Østerbro

I wish I'd bummed-out more often,
left showering and shaving as something
for people in the army to concern themselves with.
    I wish I'd left a simple tribute,
a smile or the meaningless milage of the sparest of
    spare change

down on the finite stop-signs of pool table and
    bastard-hard bar counter.
I wish I'd played that game more often, killed her lover,
left her behind when she expected me to push her in
    the bonnet.
This isn't 1974 I told her, I'd rather wear slacks than jeans.

The morning's more bummed out than me
it's nice to see. No, it's not nice to see,
me and this city's mornings could've been real real close
if my heart was soft like a maid's

The Coaling Towers of Ohio

Horse-hoof symphonies of Ohio,
lead your yellow school-buses to our
stern and dignified tribal elders

who called to arms in sepia
before English, French, and German rifles
flashed their lens first - a lens without an eye,

shutting narratives forever.
John Sanderson's our eyes, our hopes, our tribal chief,
frames pale as wisdom that sinks sunset into this blessed
    rusty suit

Inspired by the photography of John Sanderson

April Blue

Outside your head, inside your head,
I'm not sure where planets are bigger,

where Earth stays naked and obedient as it is, so far
    today.
I'm not sure where dreams hide all day before they
    meander

into your head, are they smoking cigarettes by a wall
where trains roar like Roman lions to carry food, oil,
    and tirades of tamed

automobiles across their steely spines -
across lands photographs

baptize, so they turn to horrible angry virgins?
I'm not sure.

Coming home, I've never been so beautifully alone,
cobalt electricity buzzing around river-thick evergreen
    leaves

in the sudden voltage
of April blue. I do know of course, where everything
    in you head comes from,

I'll let you know
after church on Sunday, or maybe that day you finally
    beat me at pool

Song for Ned Maddrell

December 27th 1974

Gales of Gaels as fallen warriors flicker different stations,
under muck, acoustic and primitive in their transmissions,

this lexicon doesn't lean on subway walls -
this lexicon stubbing half-dead cigarettes while rapists
    and pushers run riot -

not on this station.
The crabs scurry to shore. Sound and vision

wash away to sea just for a while,
you, Ned Maddrell, are turning scarce, closing down -
    just for now, not forever;

Oie vie
as hee'm oo, Ned Maddrell.

A Collection of Letters From the Alphabet
Assembled In Certain Orders #4, #30, #19

I need to be placid, as stone is simple.
Father forgive me,
did you hear me?

Oh goodness no, did I say stoned?
This dull volley of petroleum several of my mouths
make sure my sisters hate, (they really hate me for my
    songs),

my brothers hated more the night the movie screen of
    cop car lights
spat across the hardness of the moon
making me limp - he's no doctor, is he? they inquired,
    moving away really slow...

my body's weapon is the harness of the weasel wolf
and weeping cockroach. Mags and Luigi and the seven-
    string guitar picker
share milk, cookies, and the wisdom of a jackdaw who
    likes to sleep on my chimney

on stopping off from France.
Dawn arrives - a furious nudge on the clock's elderly
    sinners,
dawn departs, the train is full of projections of an
    ancient's age

of beautiful things, like prams and kids and toys that
    made it over the line
before the missiles arrived and the man in the chair sat
    there, nursed his coffee,
knew he'd hang and his people would write books to
    change everything

his philosophies had made him - that afternoon, human
    being
hacked to shreds on an alphabet's jagged remorse.
How did the doctor know the difference between an
    honorary degree

and a sliver of silver from the shillings who agreed
all was nothing except me?
naked like a stone ocean refused to let warm (or warn)

that things were coming, bad and screwed-up things the
    priest shrugged his shoulders at,
grabbing the weak little boy who maybe now and then
stepped over the line. St. Christopher carried that boy
    further,

in fact he won a bronze medal recently
in a triathlon,
talking, walking, doing his share of less than nothing;

I remembered him
sleeping on my couch
in the electrics of a stormy year

On the Road Again

I poke my stick in the moon's watery face, then apologize

-Jim Harrison

Teenagers carrying vegetable sacks
nigh-on shoulder-high -

there are no hard-shoulders road-side
in crisis-points of lands,

only those like crucifixions
under tilting heads.

The language is green, soiled, greasy-thumbed,
it communicates to the nearest dollar

and it is men who scuffle for dividends.
I question why no-one here smokes cigars.

I am naive,
I take my head from books

and read
the ways of the road,

finishing typing at a quarter to three
when the booming thump

of tribal drum
owns my wallet. Tonight, something hums in its
    spectres of azure,

its face and dream outshining sun
in a time of winds urging my curtain's

baby-faced Moses,
which eternity has billowed smoke and billowed sorrow
    waiting for

First We Take Mesopotamia, Then We Take New Mexico

The rook this morning draws

                                        its soot-tipped arms
            and waits for the rain.

                    There is no story, there is only history.

Horns beep and whoosh past,

                    the postman's silent next morning
            that followed solar-systems from nights

                    and wing-spans before.

The stories in the soaking bag may

                    form in sudden shapes on a stone-
hearted ground.

They don't ever ask if they should wait for the rain;
                    why would they?

                                        devils and darkness
exist beneath the tongue

                    migrating south in the summer.

                                        They soon knew how to take

sound from word,

do it so hard,

so relentlessly that

Mesopotamia

burned and burned

all that summer.
A number of witnesses remain.

The rook holds its council.

New Mexico has a lot in store - the rook says to a passing
well-wisher.

its highways

are laces dangling

from sprinters' sneakers,

its moonlight -

headlamps

from passing ghosts

Damon Harris Sang for Me

The claws of the clothesline tree
snap each of the moon's senses.

A window that makes districts of me, I tame
before I approach, seeing ornaments of women

through the ages.
One is a queen who sailed a steamboat,

kept Tennessee Williams'
tongue and teeth from approaching that liquor bottle.

One
is a Goddess - Celtic, African - I'm not sure -

she's leering towards that moon
at war with a clothesline tree

saying to me
she's of sky rather than sea. That's everything I see

until that cow-horned car pulls in,
anger and greed poison its seats,

and as its plagues pass in to several houses
I wonder if those ornaments are immortal or from
    shopping aisles in 1980s places

my aunt took me to,
waiting for the suburb's buses soon to merge like moon
    and spindly trees outside.

Everyone is dead inside these houses.
Nightshade fits into dimples on a stone-hearted moon,

I walk through that milk-powder debris
listening to age old-tales from Greece, from Egypt's sands,

I listen to the real Temptations, now a thousand times
    one hundred years old,
Damon Harris still my favourite, the lamb that took a
    silver sword's glinted blow,

bending that sword
like it was nothing, shapes of music that sunshine ignites

burning nightshade
from moon's shivering face

Someone

Someone hears you,
someone sees you, some child passing in its parents' car,
an eerie time-clenched glance.

Someone smiles when you stand aside
letting them slither past first,
some lovers

smooching down a lane-way
full of clanging bins
looking over their shoulder smugly, at you.

Someone cries for blood,
someone for love spilled
across their hands, broken pieces of warriors

lined-up in jigsaws
in their graves.
And you look so smug,

your lover biting on your ear,
someone you knew
that wasn't the one glancing away,

pale-eyed sundown glint
a narration of someone's
moonshine bedtime guilt

Bukcheong Sajanoreum (The Lion of Korea)

Arirang T.V. play, April 2023

Master sharpens blade,
he's a man no hero to me, this slayer - this man
bent to an eager satanic shape; ugly, killer, mocking;

and what you do, archaic child of muddy earth
    transmitting on my electrics,
is become the lord of the merciless, the one forgiveness
    seeks
to remove its virtue from,

all around this dance, yet separate,
where colour finds its home in simmering fire,
where morning, noon, and forever brings the lion's light

to a distance spoken in midnight's dangling heights -
I'm a proud foreigner at home, this throne
I keep after nocturne paints itself silent,

shows me the Lion's resurrection
and the semantics of fact burrowing in the myth,
the lion and the slayer

bow in tandem,
before I sell my hours to creatures who sleep - you -
those similar sunset creatures.

Bravo
maestro, this show is infinite,
like a wheel made from galaxies shaped by man and beast

Posters All Across the Block Tell Me
Your Cat is Missing

Seems like every blow-dried
one-night stand online-app lady killer
ranked by beige chinos
in p.r. agencies across the city has something to say

in modern terms,
electronic egos ablaze across the wire.
Not you - the archaic pen and paper corresponds your
    loss,
a silence louder than binary blabber.

Every lad who rides a fold-up bike to work,
schmoozes lunch from a farmer's market
and puts photos of himself on *facebook*
building villages in Africa - are welded to uselessness by

a cat who runs across a dream in front of me, stops;
    I too am invisible.
And I remember your pleas,
photostats across telegraph poles in the colon of the city,
like distress signals of yore.

The ancient cries of *Mafdet*, *Bastet* and *Sekhmet*
lurk everywhere, even taunting death itself
in the provinces, on papyrus, sun-graph, electric ego's
short-circuited distress

Oh No : Elvis Presley's Dead

So, Elvis Presley lied
about me spying for Red China. No response.
I tap my microphone, static fuzz.

Everyone at windows in rooms
in belching cities
remark that rain season came from jazz trumpets' embers -

just after dusk;
death the Spaniards brought to the Americas, has ended.
I've left my seat, heels clop like gavel falls on a sorry
    corridor

to the end of a hall where America and Europe still don't
    know how
they too could die.

I remember, Elvis Aaron Presley
out on the dark sidewalks of neon-scented poems
of restaurants we'd never been

pissing in the museum of brutalist whirring machines
when I saw sunset grow jealous,
a couple out on the beach, waiting for the world to end:
    they knew;

not Spanish themselves, though disappointed
at Elvis Aaron Presley's fall from disgrace. "Oh no,
    Elvis Presley's dead."

I never got my revenge, "try this Rioja, takes our minds
  off stuff and things and living..."

It's dawned on me that crossword clue
S - 13 across:
Schadenfreude in the corner of a room in a city

I left my newspaper lying around in
close to a window a woman stands beside
and Roy Orbison lights her cigarette

in his sad sad language.
Has it anything to sing
but murder and science and the war zones of gas
  company bills?

Plaça de l'Ajuntament, Valencia

When I dreamed three nights ago
I was three nights closer to a dream I had of you
sitting on a bench three minutes
from *Plaça de l'Ajuntament* -
three orbits from every street
I dreamed I wouldn't find you on,
awake, icicles burned in my window pane.
The planets that surround me have what I suppose
could be seen as streets - spaces where dreams of

    Moorish conquest

revolve around moon and sizzle around sun
falling to me in dust I wipe from my window pane,
that third-last Sunday dusk on *Plaça de l'Ajuntament*

Jacques Car-Oh-Whack

                              Never turn back, young soldier boy!

                                        this battle commences
under a crescent moon its insides
            fell from
                              to be sectioned off in a
      medium-sized city's high-rise car-park

that car McQueen was chasing

                                                  fell off
when his insides were as battered,
                        as destroyed as that moon's insides.
Never turn back. I'm listening to Genesis from
            1973

                  picturing my aunt's wedding photos

      sometime around this song

escaping
  escaping
                  escaping

                  so atomically

that letters and words in the multiverse were hit by the
      debris.

We have language and sound still

all-b-yit
    in unmatching

       databases of semiotic (dis)order(s).

A letter from St. Gabriel
            to the double-denim wolf-face

              beer-guts

will cast England free of that economic mess
                in 1973.

       I know. I watch the agricultural folk

   plough their upright troopers of corn.

I'm Tired Of Falling Off My Horse, I'm Tired Of Getting Back Up

From narrative to grave,
from water, growling mud,
stars squeezed from time

into a kind of death
electricity and magic
refused to spell in Latin script.

These are the alphabets
primitives made,
these are why deities cursed us, will someday understand

why that game-show host
stood tall by the chaos of Atlantis,
making families repeat every failure that burned runes
    and hieroglyphs in their beds

The Man Who Writes the Songs About Freight Trains

After death comes music, before death comes an image,
a conception immaculate among clicking ballast
I've heard - at milepoint 17 - after death,
or this change of being who

walks on water in the creep of distance
following this image to water's magic blur -
the man who writes the songs about freight trains
parks his Plymouth Fury near that gas station diner.

I read a map the sky rains on sleepers for me,
find it's seven minutes drive from here, after death,
    before death,
a liner stalled on loop-lines between.
Locomotive 075 had its share of dramas before - it waits
    as a tractable stallion would wait

Sherlockstown, County Kildare. Summer 2022

Photograph of Women in a Japanese Swimming Pool, 1931

From the back page of the first edition of the Irish Press

Sunflower soldiers limply arched in meatless grass
are silent on this matter, October's

snare drum feet bleeding on the tin can street
mean little to me, my daughters, their windpipes among
    many ports of matter,

unaware, unconcerned how
Joseph and Mary take their rhythms through my neon
    ligatures

who ask silly things in languages
Babel destroyed

as Seraphim arrives.
There is jewellery in her bladder, wine,

a confession she makes
I've abandoned for other Gods of war,

blunt acoustics wriggling off her tongues
and daughters'

surgical stance on sunflowers
limp on soaking grass, not troubled about language right
    now,

the absolutions of sun
on the stern wrinkled beach

are a good distraction
for my dogs and I, on days like these,

worried about girls throughout time and space
and the brittle shapes that shatter

in the jigsaws
of drowning place

The Thing, It Has Come to Cripple Me

A sad sad idiot is
sunset's icy penance
who awaits me at birth,
for I will know of many things

after my tongue's aversion to wisdom,
or a fisherman who sought shorelines
that math and prayer seek in mirrors
shattered on its spines -

he, who stands beneath the sorrow of stone and silent
    bridge
spoke thar first frost of summer
not long after moonlight kidnapped fire,
and Jack stood there in a fear

I'd never seen such a smart old man be numb from

Binn Éadair, 20th of April

For Rosa and Hassen Abadlia

Thursday's its own dominion now,
unharmed in pressing moments
damaged days or snake-tongued seconds,
simple amnesties of Thursday - beaming down

from the visage of Jesus-mothered rocks
our wobbling harbour slows its aches for;
we raise our glasses, stare out to sea - this could be
    Cantabria,
Biscay, Roscoff, he muses - she concurs, tipping
    coca-cola's abyss

towards a terrestrial light,
April's voice
carving psalms on steady sea-bound wood;
this place Provence watches dance in its yelling
    tomorrows -

but, holds back its needs for now;
we, citizens of splendid permanence,
jazzy comfort an extra-terrestrial sound - for unbound
    theology

What Did the Book of Leviticus Say About Shellfish?

What did the Book of Leviticus say about eating shellfish,
a lose and lonely homily
in high-rise bandages of light like insects coming for
    revenge

on the boys who pulled their legs off? .
when we sat there in 1989
two years more we'd wait for the soldiers to numb the
    fires of our fallen idol:

What did it say, Monsignor? that day you remembered
how to turn fish into chaff, loaves into stone, your
    chalk-mark
smudging the collar of our most demonic student, not
    saluting his inferior...

Harold at Cheviot, 1967, Benjamin
at Beaumaris, 1936

Meet me halfway, boys,
meet for a drink, some nifty sip of plonk,
meet me at dreamtime, walkabout sun-fire,
at water's lip and the holes like bloodshot eyes
pierced in the lungs of the cage,
meet me Harold when those lungs have had enough,
meet me Benjamin, when those eyes have grown tired
of the foreigners' fetish for blood.
Meet me, boys, come meet me, I know a nice laid-back bar
down 'round Gippsland way

The Boy

He's an alien explosion,
laughter his entrails,
his music is a chair he rocks to his perfect storm in,
laughter, his enemy, his seated animal, his indigo shape
    a departure from an ideal of self
our 1960s seers experimented in, that their tapestry of
    tongues swallowed his being
sending him here to me, today, this gut-lavished
    Autumn day,
deconstructed boy's
surroundings imitate by whirling their fingertips beside
    their craniums -
he's my poem now
and they cannot hurt him, his laughter has almost killed
    him today,
bricolage those locked-up poets lost
in love letters to a hooker on a spaceship specifically
    dated to within inches
of their leaden-days,
the boy, sitting near me, not near enough for me to
    assimilate,
bring tea, lukewarm kinship efforts to

"For the Collection of All Dead and Worn
Out Animals, Contact Animals Collection
Services Ltd."

Dead pigs
full of grace
keep peaceful hours the abattoir's clock

ticks and tocks in fault-lines of shimmering heartbreakers
who drive Sunday's average cars
past to eat sandwiches and discuss their daughter's
    wedding

to an up and coming local business-man who inherited
his late father's animal collection service.
On their way

to hope and pray
in pencil thin mustache,
roads of death flash in shocking silver

formerly from purses agonised
with ten-pence pieces;
the sanguine nations of the twisted hour–

serene
un-hacked pigs
legal, tender; the loneliness of the trucks of nobody,

driving through puddles no-one avoids
so they can make their own collage of absolution
on roads

that pigs made poems
of carnage drip into poems of heroes
one heartbeat back in the dangling past

Yvonne

I blame myself.
In the 16 days I held out at the Alamo the only thing I
    could call a song
was the single drip that timed itself like Chinese water
    torture
from a tap no-one fixed,

something I remembered from my local swimming pool
when a tap stood there dribbling since 2003
like a simple child with its pants around its ankles in a
    bathroom
in a railway station in the wide-open colon

of the seldom emptied midwest.
I blame myself.
As I watched Jimmy leave and turn handbrake skids
to the amusement of a few nurses in the carpark

I switched to Radio Veteris.
Yvonne tuned her mask meanwhile, to the other side of
    Cygnus.
Someone who is beautiful and loved must die,
Yvonne lives on

haunting h.r. departments and solemn-whitewashed
    sinners
on the spectrums of the sixth floor,
lift opening like a sardine tin to weld me in
her stone-cold suburban sins.

Guess I'll wax up my saddle
before sun goes down, make a technicolor sign of the
    cross
that impales her in its ten-mile shadow,
Yvonne more gone than a gopher's ribcage in a blizzard.

I gave what holy water I had to my stallion,
sins I had I left with her,
leaving her to drown
on the sticky barren land, somewhere very east of her
    lover's shabby grave

Photograph of a Delaware & Hudson Boxcar, Mid 1970s : Door Left Open

My fingerprint on space
that day's edges wander :
I meander
through a sack of mail - mute and docile, what it reveals
to old ladies due-west of wise health,
orange crates' nibbled sins little boys
found passe even when Little Richard
still believed in Heaven and Hell -
I slide along to diesel's dreary dream,
a landscape ephemeral America knitted tattoos in,
this space a camera's corpse maims in winter's music,
music hurried on notes of frost,
the blood-rust choirs gurgling in rivers
in towns where sheriffs call themselves Sam.
The boxcar rivets stitched like nylon lives
make denim maps of man's decline,
I hurry dusk's cinnamon sagging
as a pointless remembrance

The Smoke, The Moon, The Soft Soft Rain

Clanranald Road and Clanawley Road, Dublin.

March, 3rd, 2023

Hollywood connections
lock shut - lives who
fade soon
as camera pans away;

not smoke,
not moon,
not soft soft rain, all of these sparks to my senses,
alphabets that speak of stolen angels, hidden in dusk-
    dusted blues;

Friday's flight to Saturday's lights
shields this sidewalk -
look at me -
holding out, camera still suspicious;

everyday I set myself a few simple tasks -
get that hairy ass outside kid,
do some shopping,
grab some coffee, French bread-rolls hot from the oven,

returning from the track
a week before the plagues of lighting struck,
lying low in Nice and Cannes,
writing-paper curling at its sides.

When the cheque arrived in Grace and Rainier's second-
     favourite bar
he said, "let's go halves", I went full and damned his eyes,
those green lizard eyes which said so much and meant
     so little;
he texted later to say we had nothing in common -

I didn't argue -
his twitchy fear of all-things warm
like a post office-clerk or serial killer
evading everything in this life except

those fingerprints God gave him in 1978.
I met a girl called Miss Amanda Jones soon after.
By 1969 Hell's Angels
were muscling round her boss's

turf as well,
collar deep in the devil's hymn-sheet.
I never seen Amanda or her maid
Miss Tiffany again, after her Bugatti broke down fleeing
     the *Guardia Civil,*

she flashed her legs and the Hell's Angels
came and she hopped on, Amanda waiting behind
to accept her faithlessness. She called me long-distance,
said "grab a shovel and dig deep as Hell at that Joshua
     Tree."

Today I read of her swinging light-bulb from a cracked
     ceiling scenario,
milkmen prowl streets shrouded in the end of days.

Dancing days will soon be here again,
I look at the railway tracks, the sun is rising in 15 hours
time,

Nilfisk flasks ebbing tea in the avalanche of dirty white
vans
like sea bullies harbor
in the mold of wild-child
and the pigeons in the park.

Days run shorter - don't I know - when Summer grows;
It's a tragedy too, how much love comes through our
windows
in the morning, breathtaking blues of fading faces
in cafes, in Montmartre - Summer like that old man

face-first on the pavement,
ambulance neatly tucked in behind him
on the sun's stomach so heavy
it could never rise again with any meaning -

buried by the dirge of evening,
stealing angels' names from my dog and me.
No-one steals even a shilling this evening -
from the smoke, the moon,

especially the soft, soft rain.
I think that's what's stands us apart
from the salesmen
and from the murderers -

no-one steals nothing
in a concrete palace blessed by the blues,
they reach their palms to the dreams of cedars,
drink their water from the cups of the Lily. This is
    everything we need - no more

Joshua's on the Cusp of Sales and Marketing Success

It comes to pass whether you believe in God or Math
that Joshua follows systems, illuminations, towns and
    cars and people who take cold showers,
all too, must come to pass -
that Joshua's kin heard singers sing
"I'm off doing what Lord Kitchener wants me to do,
    are you man enough too?",
that Joshua's price when it comes to pass
is to chat with my wife and I
hoping a sky-blue shirt strangled in a cocaine-white collar
will seduce us into parting with our senses.
No, Joshua. No it won't.
Joshua still can't explain
that he knows what
capital guaranteed investment actually means,
narcotics and narcissus winding those
wrist-watches in his dreams around our throats
into the cackle of our screams.
And the rats are just rats, that's what Gods program
    them to be,
and the waiters are just waiters, that's what Gods
    program them to be,
and poems are just poems, that's what Gods program
    them to be,
and Joshua's just a barbarian, a murderer without a creed,
that's what Mammon programmed him to be...

Blood Water, Torrevieja

Pornography is so bland,
nuclear war is so bland,
thoughts of infinite torment as Hell rages all around me,
so bland, so *passé*...

After a while, frogspawn appeared near the riverbank,
trains stuttered past,
someone spoke about Bobby Sands and Margaret Thatcher
on the radio. I knew life would go down-hill one second
    past midnight.

Sitting oceanside, I remember;
bloodiest dream a Spanish sailor dreamed
comes knocking at my toes,
sunset maims me in each bullet - silver, lead, close enough
    to gold, I guess,

but I have bred and bled my blood
to seep inside no history,
no cherub's effigy
washing its wound in this giggling water

There Are Worse Things Than
Eternal Damnation

I will renounce this magic and repent
-Christopher Marlowe

With the stale and sorrowful mass
of returning actors after Hollywood smiled
and said "no"
and death forgot to snatch them

from the dank and cloudy lungs of the St. James Hotel,
every line spoken and rewound
garrottes the essence
of their cigarette-battered faces.

A stopped clock gets it right twice in 24 hours,
a typewriter's weak insipid ticking -
tongue-less most days.
These are things worse than eternal damnation,

a clock's teasing tocks,
a window that lets every city know
how far they did not come;
it is perhaps righteous and just

John Doyle is from County Kildare in Ireland, and lives in Dublin with his wife and their two dogs. Finding inspiration in Americana, cobalt April dusk, and endless freight trains tingling on the barren horizon, these poems focus on the undercurrents of the familiar - like barely audible conversations on white-washed porches and tyremarks on red clay edges of highways - or what Doyle likes to call, "those important things..."

This project was made possible, in part, by generous support from the Osage Arts Community.

Osage Arts Community provides temporary time, space and support for the creation of new artistic works in a retreat format, serving creative people of all kinds — visual artists, composers, poets, fiction and nonfiction writers. Located on a 152-acre farm in an isolated rural mountainside setting in Central Missouri and bordered by ¾ of a mile of the Gasconade River, OAC provides residencies to those working alone, as well as welcoming collaborative teams, offering living space and workspace in a country environment to emerging and mid-career artists. For more information, visit us at www.osageac.org

Osage Arts Community